THIS BOOK IS ALL ABOUT

_____

Birth Date

Birth Location

Adoption Date

Adoption Location

Birth Weight & Length

Lovingly Recorded By

TABLE OF CONTENTS

4

IN THE BEGINNING

WHY WE DECIDED ADOPTION WAS RIGHT FOR US

_____

_____

_____

_____

_____

_____

THE FIRST PEOPLE WE TOLD ABOUT OUR DECISION TO ADOPT

_____

_____

_____

_____

_____

HOW THE FAMILY FELT ABOUT ADOPTION

_____

_____

_____

_____

_____

We Chose ☐ Domestic ☐ International Adoption Because:

_____
_____
_____
_____

Where You Were Born And How We Found You:

_____
_____
_____
_____
_____

Where & What We Did When We First Met:

_____
_____
_____
_____
_____
_____

What You Mean To Us:

_____
_____
_____
_____

How We Got Ready For Your Arrival:

_____
_____
_____
_____
_____
_____

Siblings & Pets Excited To Meet You:

Siblings	Age
_____	_____
_____	_____
_____	_____
_____	_____

Pets

_____
_____
_____

ADDITIONAL NOTES

THE PROCESS

USE THIS SPACE TO ENTER THE IMPORTANT DATES IN THE ADOPTION PROCESS

Example: choosing the provider, home visits, first meeting, introduction, etc.

GiRAFFES

ZEBRAS

SAFARi TOURS

LIONS

DATE

WHAT HAPPENED

DATE THE ADOPTION
PROCESS BEGAN

DATE THE JUDGE
SAID, "YES"!

TOTAL LENGTH OF
TIME THE ADOPTION
PROCESS TOOK

ADOPTION DAY

A D O P T I O N   D A Y   P H O T O
(4x6 photo)

_____

date

_____

age

location

A D O P T I O N   D A Y   P H O T O
(4x6 photo)

presiding judge

_____
weather

_____
favorite toy

_____
famous actor/actress

_____
major news story

_____
current president

_____
cost of a stamp

_____
popular movie

_____
cost of a movie ticket

_____
popular song

_____
cost of gas/gallon

_____
cost of a cup of coffee

_____
cost of milk/gallon

NOTES FROM FAMILY and FRIENDS

NOTES FROM FAMILY and FRIENDS

FOREVER FAMILY

MY FOREVER FAMILY

PHOTO OF ME
(4x6 photo)

PHOTO WITH SIBLINGS
(4x6 photo)

MY FOREVER FAMILY

PHOTO WITH MOMMY
(trim photo to fit)

PHOTO WITH DADDY
(trim photo to fit)

PHOTO WITH FOREVER FAMILY
(4x6 photo)

MY "BIRTH FAMILY" TREE

PARENT NAME   PARENT NAME

....

SIBLINGS

_____

_____

GRANDPARENTS   GRANDPARENTS

_____   _____

_____   _____

_____

AUNTS & UNCLES   AUNTS & UNCLES

....

....

MY "ADOPTIVE FAMILY" TREE

PARENT NAME

PARENT NAME

SIBLINGS

GRANDPARENTS

GRANDPARENTS

AUNTS & UNCLES

AUNTS & UNCLES

23

ALL ABOUT MOMMY

FULL NAME

BIRTHDAY

WHERE I GREW UP

MY FAVORITE CHILDHOOD MEMORIES

MY INTERESTS & HOBBIES

WHAT I WANT YOU TO KNOW ABOUT ME

L♥ve Letter From Mommy

NEVER FORGET . . .

MY DREAM FOR YOU . .

ALL ABOUT DADDY

_____   _____
FULL NAME   BIRTHDAY

WHERE I GREW UP

MY FAVORITE CHILDHOOD MEMORIES

MY INTERESTS & HOBBIES

WHAT I WANT YOU TO KNOW ABOUT ME

Love Letter From Daddy

NEVER FORGET . . .

MY DREAM FOR YOU . .

12 MONTHS

1ST MONTH PHOTO
(4x6 photo)

1ST MONTH---->

with my forever family

THIS MONTH'S PERSONALITY

- [ ] quiet
- [ ] loud
- [ ] calm
- [ ] cuddly

- [ ] fussy
- [ ] silly
- [ ]
- [ ]

OTHER NEW THINGS THIS MONTH

Example: sounds, expressions, food, places, words, etc.

NEW FIRSTS

FAVORITE TOY(S)

THINGS I ENJOYED

BEDTIME ROUTINE

DOCTOR VISITS

ADDITIONAL NOTES

2ND MONTH----->

with my forever family

2ND MONTH PHOTO
(4x6 photo)

TOUR GUIDE

THIS MONTH'S PERSONALITY

- ☐ quiet
- ☐ loud
- ☐ calm
- ☐ cuddly

- ☐ fussy
- ☐ silly
- ☐
- ☐

OTHER NEW THINGS THIS MONTH

Example: sounds, expressions,
food, places, words, etc.

NEW FIRSTS

FAVORITE TOY(S)

THINGS I ENJOYED

BEDTIME ROUTINE

DOCTOR VISITS

ADDITIONAL NOTES

3RD MONTH PHOTO
(4x6 photo)

3RD MONTH
with my forever family

THIS MONTH'S PERSONALITY

- ☐ quiet
- ☐ loud
- ☐ calm
- ☐ cuddly

- ☐ fussy
- ☐ silly
- ☐
- ☐

OTHER NEW THINGS THIS MONTH

Example: sounds, expressions, food, places, words, etc.

BEDTIME ROUTINE

NEW FIRSTS

FAVORITE TOY(S)

THINGS I ENJOYED

DOCTOR VISITS

ADDITIONAL NOTES

4ᵀᴴ MONTH PHOTO
(4x6 photo)

TOUR GUIDE

4ᵀᴴ MONTH----→

with my forever family

THIS MONTH'S PERSONALITY

- ☐ quiet
- ☐ loud
- ☐ calm
- ☐ cuddly

- ☐ fussy
- ☐ silly
- ☐
- ☐

OTHER NEW THINGS THIS MONTH

Example: sounds, expressions, food, places, words, etc.

NEW FIRSTS

FAVORITE TOY(S)

THINGS I ENJOYED

BEDTIME ROUTINE

DOCTOR VISITS

ADDITIONAL NOTES

ADDITIONAL NOTES

5TH MONTH----→

with my forever family

5TH MONTH PHOTO
(4x6 photo)

THIS MONTH'S PERSONALITY

☐ quiet   ☐ fussy

☐ loud   ☐ silly

☐ calm   ☐

☐ cuddly   ☐

NEW FIRSTS

FAVORITE TOY(S)

THINGS I ENJOYED

OTHER NEW THINGS THIS MONTH

Example: sounds, expressions,
food, places, words, etc.

BEDTIME ROUTINE

DOCTOR VISITS

ADDITIONAL NOTES

6TH MONTH PHOTO
(4x6 photo)

6TH MONTH
with my forever family

THIS MONTH'S PERSONALITY

- ☐ quiet
- ☐ loud
- ☐ calm
- ☐ cuddly
- ☐ fussy
- ☐ silly
- ☐
- ☐

OTHER NEW THINGS THIS MONTH

Example: sounds, expressions,
food, places, words, etc.

BEDTIME ROUTINE

NEW FIRSTS

FAVORITE TOY(S)

THINGS I ENJOYED

DOCTOR VISITS

ADDITIONAL NOTES

7TH MONTH PHOTO
(4x6 photo)

7TH MONTH ----->
with my forever family

THIS MONTH'S PERSONALITY

- ☐ quiet
- ☐ loud
- ☐ calm
- ☐ cuddly
- ☐ fussy
- ☐ silly
- ☐
- ☐

OTHER NEW THINGS THIS MONTH

Example: sounds, expressions, food, places, words, etc.

BEDTIME ROUTINE

NEW FIRSTS

FAVORITE TOY(S)

THINGS I ENJOYED

DOCTOR VISITS

ADDITIONAL NOTES

8TH MONTH ----->

with my forever family

8TH MONTH PHOTO
(4x6 photo)

TOUR GUIDE

THIS MONTH'S PERSONALITY

- ☐ quiet
- ☐ loud
- ☐ calm
- ☐ cuddly

- ☐ fussy
- ☐ silly
- ☐
- ☐

NEW FIRSTS

FAVORITE TOY(S)

THINGS I ENJOYED

OTHER NEW THINGS THIS MONTH

Example: sounds, expressions,
food, places, words, etc.

BEDTIME ROUTINE

DOCTOR VISITS

ADDITIONAL NOTES

9TH MONTH PHOTO
(4x6 photo)

9TH MONTH----→
with my forever family

THIS MONTH'S PERSONALITY

- ☐ quiet
- ☐ loud
- ☐ calm
- ☐ cuddly
- ☐ fussy
- ☐ silly
- ☐
- ☐

OTHER NEW THINGS THIS MONTH

Example: sounds, expressions,
food, places, words, etc.

NEW FIRSTS

FAVORITE TOY(S)

THINGS I ENJOYED

BEDTIME ROUTINE

DOCTOR VISITS

ADDITIONAL NOTES

10ᵀᴴ MONTH PHOTO
(4x6 photo)

TOUR GUIDE

10TH MONTH

with my forever family

THIS MONTH'S PERSONALITY

- ☐ quiet
- ☐ loud
- ☐ calm
- ☐ cuddly
- ☐ fussy
- ☐ silly
- ☐
- ☐

OTHER NEW THINGS THIS MONTH

Example: sounds, expressions,
food, places, words, etc.

NEW FIRSTS

FAVORITE TOY(S)

THINGS I ENJOYED

BEDTIME ROUTINE

DOCTOR VISITS

ADDITIONAL NOTES

11TH MONTH ---->

with my forever family

11TH MONTH PHOTO
(4x6 photo)

THIS MONTH'S PERSONALITY

- ☐ quiet
- ☐ loud
- ☐ calm
- ☐ cuddly
- ☐ fussy
- ☐ silly
- ☐
- ☐

OTHER NEW THINGS THIS MONTH

Example: sounds, expressions,
food, places, words, etc.

BEDTIME ROUTINE

NEW FIRSTS

FAVORITE TOY(S)

THINGS I ENJOYED

DOCTOR VISITS

ADDITIONAL NOTES

12TH MONTH PHOTO
(4x6 photo)

12TH MONTH
with my forever family

THIS MONTH'S PERSONALITY

- ☐ quiet
- ☐ loud
- ☐ calm
- ☐ cuddly
- ☐ fussy
- ☐ silly
- ☐
- ☐

NEW FIRSTS

FAVORITE TOY(S)

THINGS I ENJOYED

OTHER NEW THINGS THIS MONTH

Example: sounds, expressions, food, places, words, etc.

BEDTIME ROUTINE

DOCTOR VISITS

ADDITIONAL NOTES

MY HAND & MY FOOT

Trace my hand and foot on ADOPTION DAY

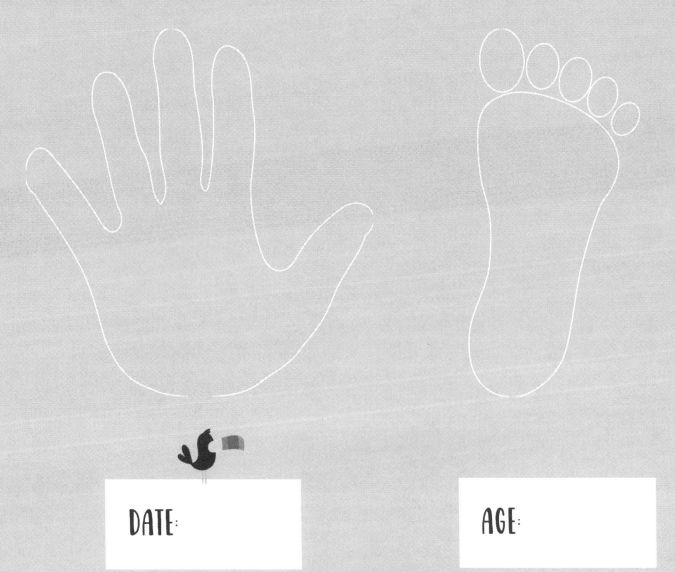

DATE:

AGE:

MY HAND & MY FOOT

Trace again 1 YEAR later

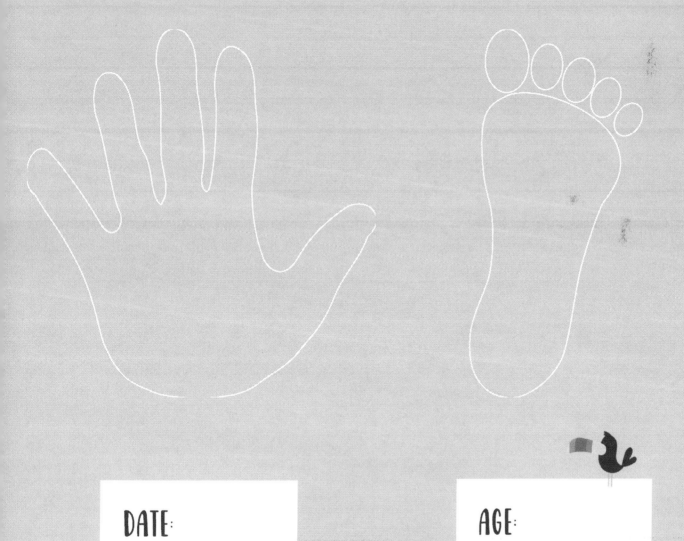

DATE:

AGE:

My Favorite Books/Movies

More of My Favorite Books/Movies

1ST YEAR PHOTO CHECKLIST

INFANT

- ○ 1st BATH
- ○ 1ST FEEDING
- ○ 1ST DOCTOR VISIT
- ○ 1ST HAIRCUT
- ○ LEARNING TO CRAWL
- ○ 1ST TIME STANDING
- ○ GIVING KISSES
- ○ FAVORITE TOYS
- ○ 1ST STEP
- ○ 1ST TOOTH
- ○ 1ST BIRTHDAY
- ○ 1ST CHRISTMAS, EASTER, HALLOWEEN

OLDER CHILD

- ○ 1st DAY OF SCHOOL
- ○ 1ST BIRTHDAY CELEBRATION
- ○ NEW BEDROOM
- ○ FAVORITE TOYS
- ○ WITH FAMILY PET(S)
- ○ HOBBIES
- ○ DANCING
- ○ SPORTS
- ○ VACATIONS
- ○ NEW FRIENDS
- ○ CHORES
- ○ 1ST CHRISTMAS, EASTER, HALLOWEEN

OTHER PHOTO IDEAS

- ○
- ○
- ○
- ○

- ○
- ○
- ○
- ○

PHOTO GALLERY

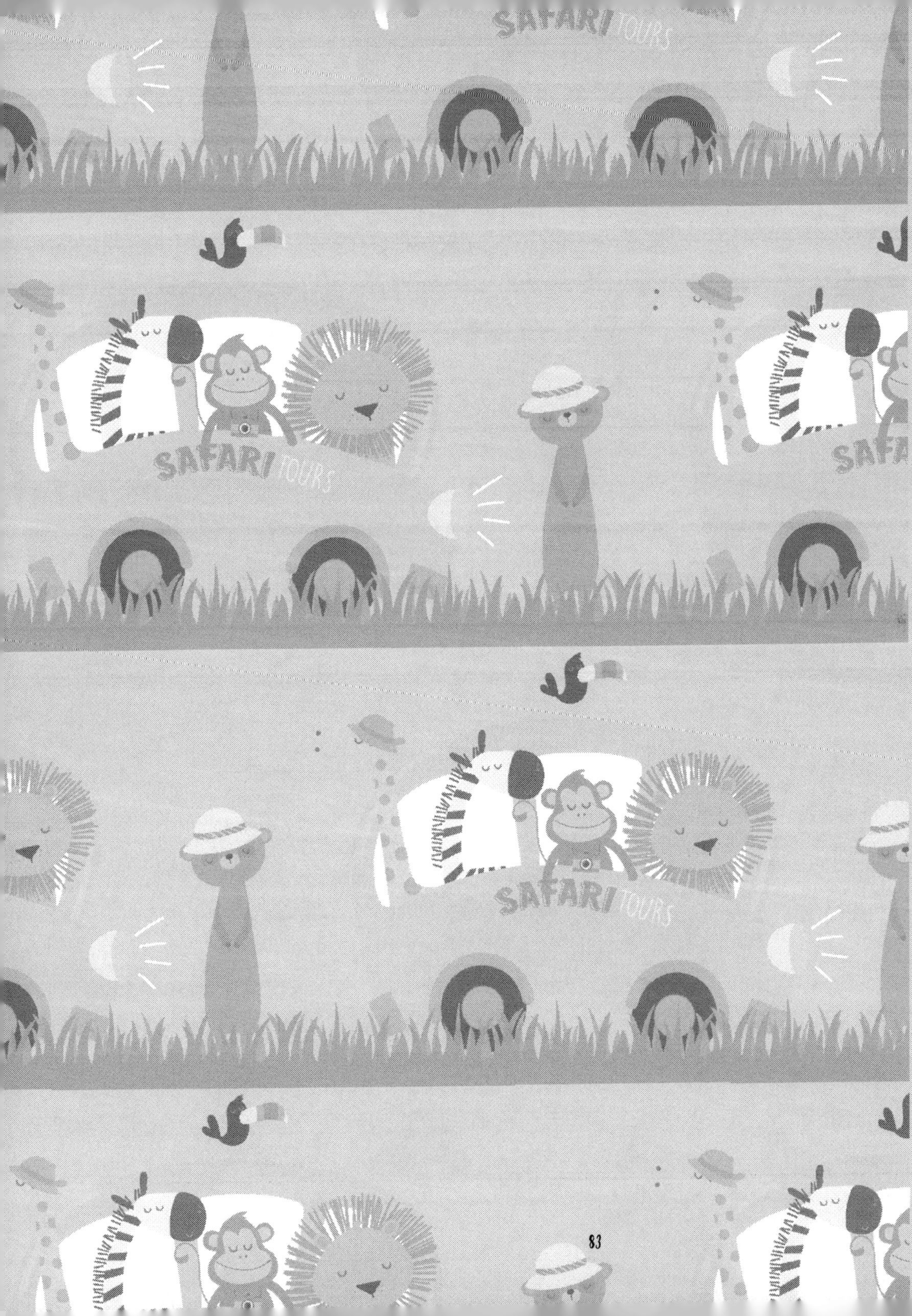

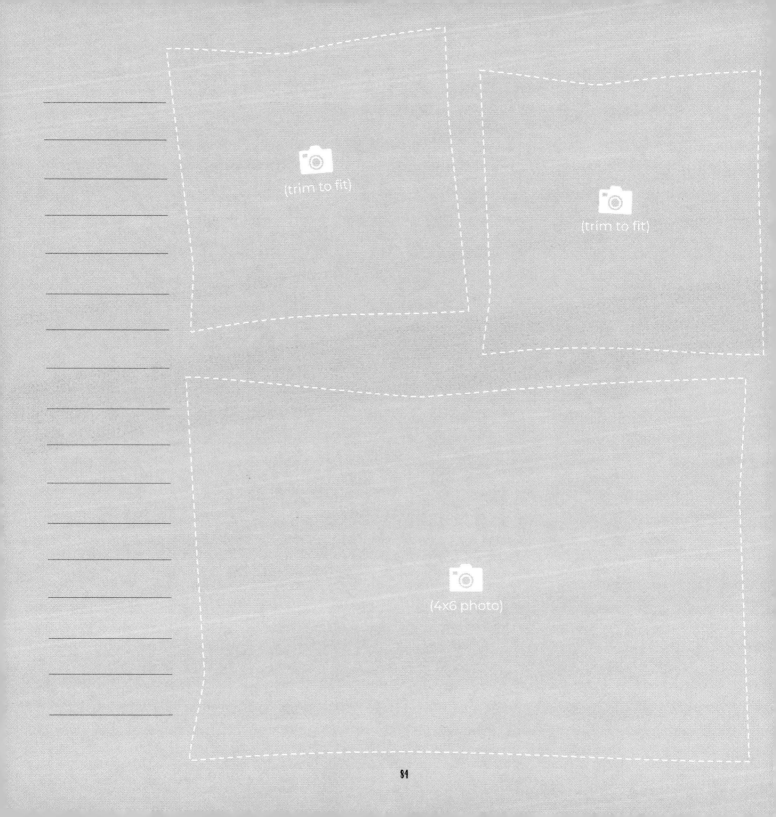

(trim to fit)

(trim to fit)

(4x6 photo)

(4x6 photo)

(trim to fit)

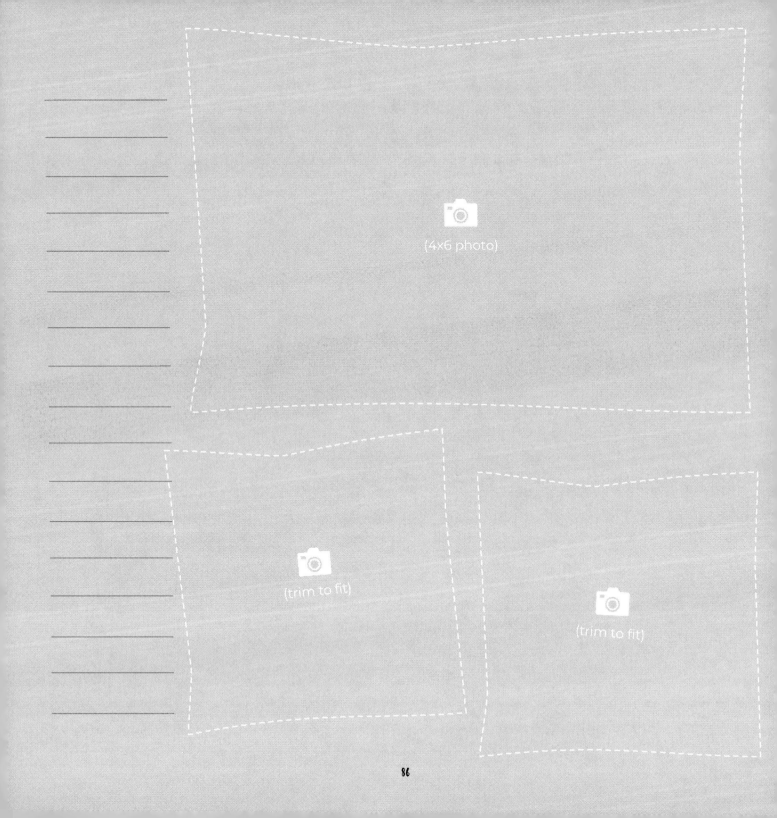

(4x6 photo)

(trim to fit)

(trim to fit)

(trim to fit)

(trim to fit)

(4x6 photo)

_____

_____

_____

_____

_____

_____

_____

_____

_____

_____

_____

(4x6 photo)

(trim to fit)

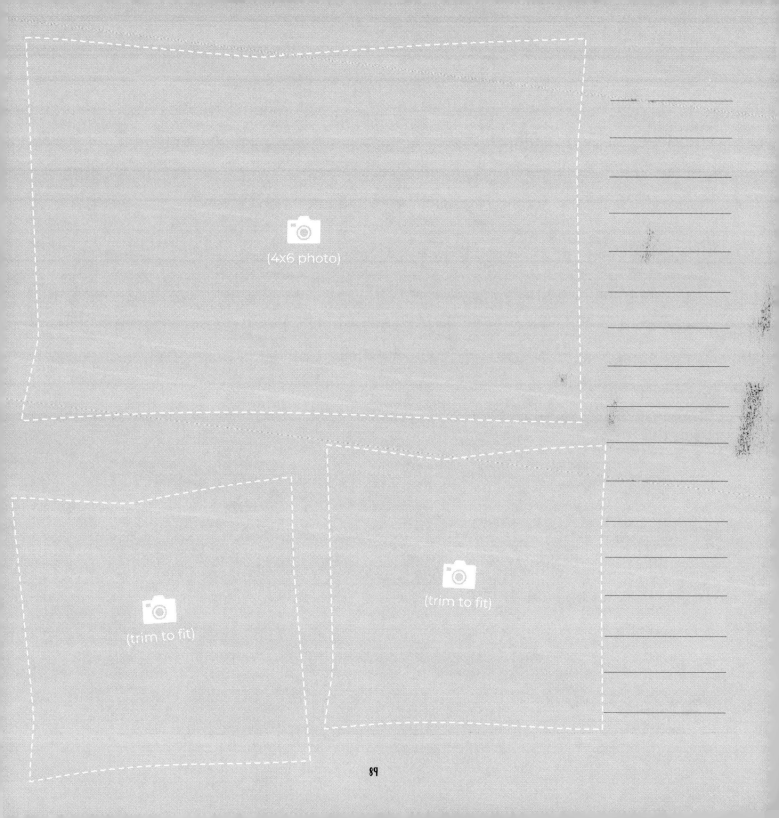

(4x6 photo)

(trim to fit)

(trim to fit)

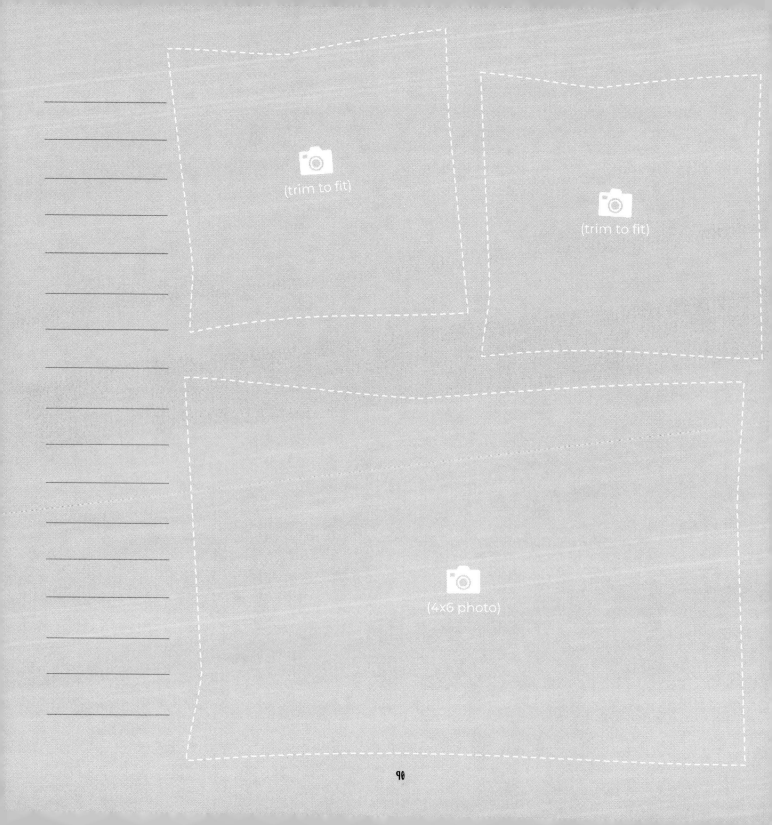

(trim to fit)

(trim to fit)

(4x6 photo)

(4x6 photo)

(trim to fit)

(4x6 photo)

(trim to fit)

(trim to fit)

(trim to fit)

(trim to fit)

(4x6 photo)

Look how good I draw

other keepsakes

_____

_____

_____

_____

_____

_____

_____

_____

_____

(sample from my first haircut)

(attach a memory here)

_____
_____
_____
_____
_____
_____
_____
_____
_____
_____

other keepsakes

other keepsakes

_____

_____

_____

_____

_____

_____

_____

_____

_____

(attach a memory here)

98

ADDITIONAL NOTES

Made in the USA
Middletown, DE
27 September 2023

39476983R10057